WHY WAR HAPPENED

WHAT CAUSED THE AMERICAN REVOLUTION?

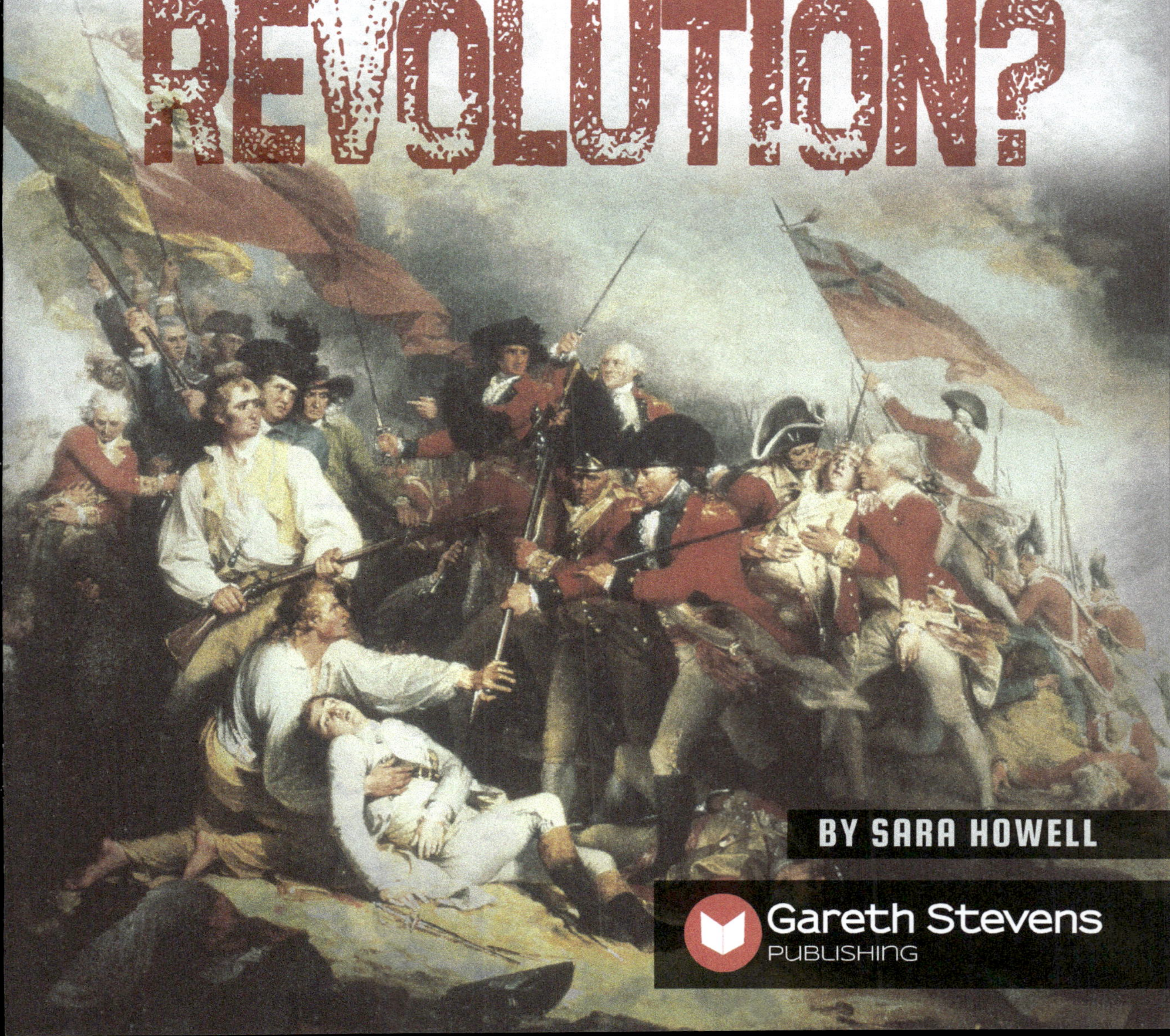

BY SARA HOWELL

Gareth Stevens
PUBLISHING

Please visit our website, www.garethstevens.com.
For a free color catalog of all our high-quality books,
call toll free 1-800-542-2595 or fax 1-877-542-2596.

Cataloging-in-Publication Data
Names: Howell, Sara.
Title: What caused the American Revolution? / Sara Howell.
Description: New York : Gareth Stevens Publishing, 2017. | Series: Why war happened | Includes index.
Identifiers: ISBN 9781482451856 (pbk.) | ISBN 9781482451795 (library bound) | ISBN 9781482451696 (6 pack)
Subjects: LCSH: United States--History--Revolution, 1775-1783--Juvenile literature. | United States--History--Revolution, 1775-1783--Causes--Juvenile literature.
Classification: LCC E208.H77 2017 | DDC 973.3--dc23

First Edition

Published in 2017 by
Gareth Stevens Publishing
111 East 14th Street, Suite 349
New York, NY 10003

Produced by Calcium
Editors: Sarah Eason and Harriet McGregor
Designer: Jessica Moon
Picture researcher: Rachel Blount

Picture credits: Cover: Getty: SuperStock (John Trumbull I painting), Shutterstock: kasha_malasha (bkgrd). Insides: Library of Congress: 17, A. Bobbett; Darley 14, Sarony & Major 25; Shutterstock: B. Brown 21, Susan Law Cain 37, Orhan Cam 43, Richard Cavalleri 26, Everett Historical 5, 7, 9, 11, 13, 19, 23, 27, 29, 31, 33, 35, 38, Iladm 45, Hein Nouwens 44, James Steidl 41.

Printed in the United States of America
CPSIA compliance information: Batch #CS16GS: For further information contact Gareth Stevens, New York, New York at 1-800-542-2595.

CONTENTS

Words in the glossary appear in **bold** type the first time they are used in the text.

CHAPTER 1

THE AMERICAN REVOLUTION

Throughout the world, wars occur for many different reasons. Some are fought over limited **natural resources**, such as oil. Others are fought over differences in religion or culture. Many wars are fought over political issues, or ideas of how a government should be run. In any war, there is usually not one single cause or event that leads to bloodshed. Wars are often the result of years of built-up dissatisfaction and conflict between two or more countries or groups of people.

Some types of wars are called revolutions. A revolution usually leads to a complete change in a country's government. Revolutions can also bring a total change in a country's religion or culture. Not all revolutions are violent. Some are peaceful but others are long and deadly wars, lasting years or even decades.

The American Revolution was a violent war. The fight between Great Britain, one of the most powerful countries in the world at the time, and a small group of British colonists, lasted just a little under eight years. It resulted in the deaths of tens of thousands of people on both sides of the conflict.

When looking at the causes of war, the American Revolution is an interesting case. For the British, both at the time of the war and now, the fighting is often considered part of a larger conflict between Great Britain and France over trade routes to the New World and access to natural resources. For the colonists, however, it was seen as a fight for independence and freedom. In this book we will examine both sides of the conflict and the events that led to war.

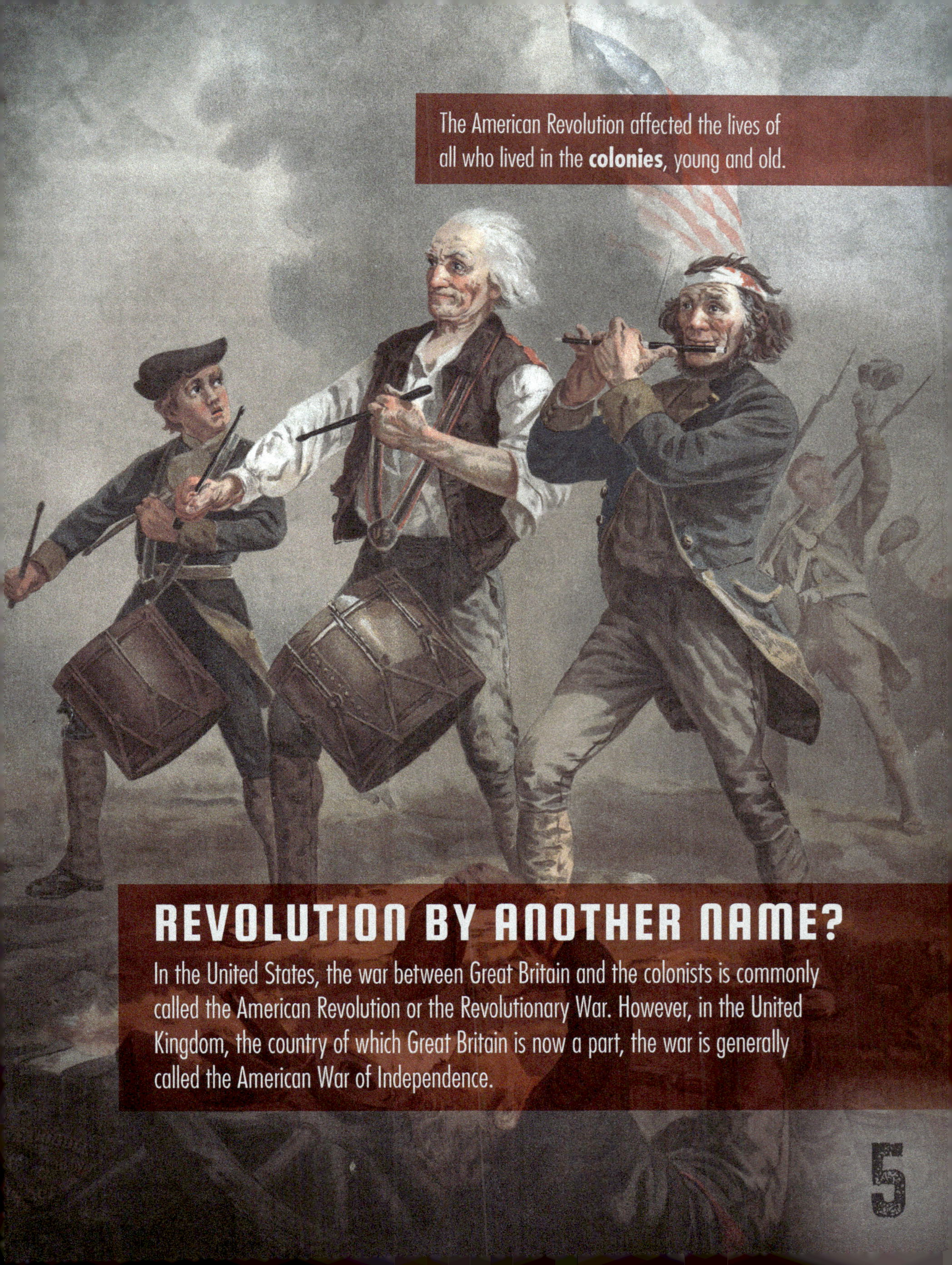

The American Revolution affected the lives of all who lived in the **colonies**, young and old.

REVOLUTION BY ANOTHER NAME?

In the United States, the war between Great Britain and the colonists is commonly called the American Revolution or the Revolutionary War. However, in the United Kingdom, the country of which Great Britain is now a part, the war is generally called the American War of Independence.

A NEW WORLD

From the fifth century through the fifteenth century, Europe was in a period named the Middle Ages, or the medieval period. This was a time of wars and the Black Death, a plague that killed at least 100 million people. As the Middle Ages came to an end around 1450, life in Europe was beginning to change. Advances in technology and agriculture allowed the population to grow. Smaller territories were combining to form larger countries ruled by powerful monarchs, or kings and queens.

For centuries, Europeans had traded with countries in Asia for goods such as spices, medicines, and silks. The network of trade routes was called the Silk Road. Near the end of the Middle Ages, the rise of the **Ottoman Empire** in central Asia made trade along the Silk Road difficult or impossible. Europeans began looking for new routes to Asia. Many explorers started to search for an ocean route between Europe and Asia.

In 1492, while attempting to find a route to Asia, Christopher Columbus (1451–1506) landed in what would become known as the New World. Although it was not the part of the world he and other explorers had been looking for, the land, which included parts of North America, South America, Central America, and nearby islands, was rich in natural resources. Over the next few hundred years, European

TRADING MORE THAN SPICES

The Silk Road stretched 6,400 miles (10,300 km) between Europe and Asia. In addition to material goods, ideas, religions, and cultures were also shared between the East and West. It is even thought that the Black Death was spread into Europe along the Silk Road.

Christopher Columbus was an Italian explorer. However, his trips to the New World were paid for by the king and queen of Spain.

countries such as France, Spain, and Portugal founded colonies there and fought over claims of ownership. In North America, though, it was England that found the most success in colonizing what is now the East Coast of the United States.

In 1607, Jamestown was founded in the Colony of Virginia. It was the first permanent English settlement in North America. Although Jamestown was later able to grow as a colony, the first several years were very difficult. Many of the original settlers died from starvation as they waited for supply ships from England. Life in North America would prove to be harsh for English settlers.

COLONIES

Over the next several decades, more settlers arrived in the New World. The area along the Atlantic coast where they settled became known as New England. As new areas of land were settled, they needed a form of structure for how they would be run and who would be in charge because England and its monarchs were so far away.

In the years before the American Revolution, England established three types of colonies in North America. These were known as royal colonies, proprietary colonies, and charter colonies. In a royal colony, which was also called a crown colony, a governor controlled the colony. The governor was not elected by the colony's members, but appointed by England's king. The crown controlled all unsold land, and was directly involved in the colony's policies. Seven of the original 13 colonies, including New York, Virginia, and New Hampshire, were royal colonies.

Proprietary colonies were areas of land given by the king to a person or family. This was usually as a reward for loyalty or service. The person, or proprietor, was responsible for governing the colony, but still answered to the king. Unlike in a royal colony, proprietors controlled unsold land. They had the authority to create courts and establish churches. Pennsylvania, Maryland, and Delaware were proprietary colonies.

In a charter colony, the king granted a **charter** to the governing body of the colony. The charter was an official agreement setting up the rules by which the colony would be run. Connecticut and Rhode Island were both charter colonies. At any time, the king could revoke, or take away, the charter and turn the colony into a royal colony. For example, the Massachusetts Bay Colony had its charter revoked in 1684.

WILLIAM PENN

In 1681, King Charles II (1630–1685) gave William Penn (1644–1718) a large piece of land in North America. The land was given as payment for a **debt** that the crown owed to Penn's father, who had served in England's Royal Navy. William Penn set up a proprietary colony called Pennsylvania. He was one of the first to encourage the English colonies to join and form a union.

William Penn maintained peaceful relations with the Native American Lenape tribes who lived in the area.

IMPORTANT TIES

From the beginning of England's settlement in North America, the relationship between those who chose to come to the New World and their home country was an important and delicate one. England, like other European countries, saw the colonies primarily as a way to make money. The New World was rich in natural resources that could be sent back to Europe.

Early settlers often went to the New World to make their fortunes. Many settlers were men who were concerned more with business ventures than with establishing a new way of life and raising families in a new land. A large number of settlers were weakened by long, difficult sea voyages with too few provisions. They were unprepared for the harsh conditions in North America and many died from starvation and malnutrition.

As time went on, many colonists began to see permanent settlement in North America as a chance to gain much more than money. Towns and cities grew, and farmers learned more about the crops that would grow well in this new

PLYMOUTH COLONY

The Pilgrims (see right) originally left England for the Netherlands before making a deal with British investors. In exchange for passage to North America, tools, and other supplies, the Pilgrims would send back natural resources, such as timber, animal furs, and fish. Though the Pilgrims at first found life difficult, several years of successful harvests and assistance from Native Americans living in the area helped Plymouth Colony became a safe and stable colony. It would later merge with the Massachusetts Bay Colony.

A 1621 feast shared by the Pilgrims and Native Americans is considered the first Thanksgiving.

environment. Colonies became a safer, more stable place to live and raise a family. With this change, however, came the idea that settlers needed to take some political control of their colonies and daily lives. This was a fundamental change in the relationship between the colonists and their home country of England.

Some settlers came to the New World looking for religious freedom. One of the most famous settlements was called Plymouth Colony, in what is now Massachusetts. It was settled in 1620, by a small group of people who wanted to separate from the Church of England. Today, these people are known as the Pilgrims.

CHAPTER 2

LIFE BEFORE THE WAR

Before the American Revolution, colonists living in North America considered themselves British. Though they lived thousands of miles from their home country of Great Britain, they were subject to the laws of the crown and their loyalty was to Great Britain. They also enjoyed the protection of Great Britain's power.

In the years leading up to the American Revolution, there were 2 million people living in the 13 colonies. Cities such as Boston and Philadelphia grew quickly, though only about 10 percent of colonists lived in large cities. Most colonists lived in rural areas and either owned or worked on farms. In the northern colonies, these were mostly small, family-run farms. The men and boys of the family planted and harvested crops. The women and girls were responsible for household duties, such as sewing, cleaning, preparing food, and taking care of the younger children.

In the southern colonies, large plantations grew crops such as tobacco. Soon tobacco was in high demand throughout Europe. Southern plantation owners brought Africans to North America to work as slaves on the plantations. The slave trade grew, and thousands of Africans were brought to the colonies each year.

During the first half of the eighteenth century, the 13 colonies became well established. While the colonies prospered and made money for Great Britain, there was little reason for the crown to interfere. However, that would soon change, and Great Britain's actions would lead the colonists closer to a revolution.

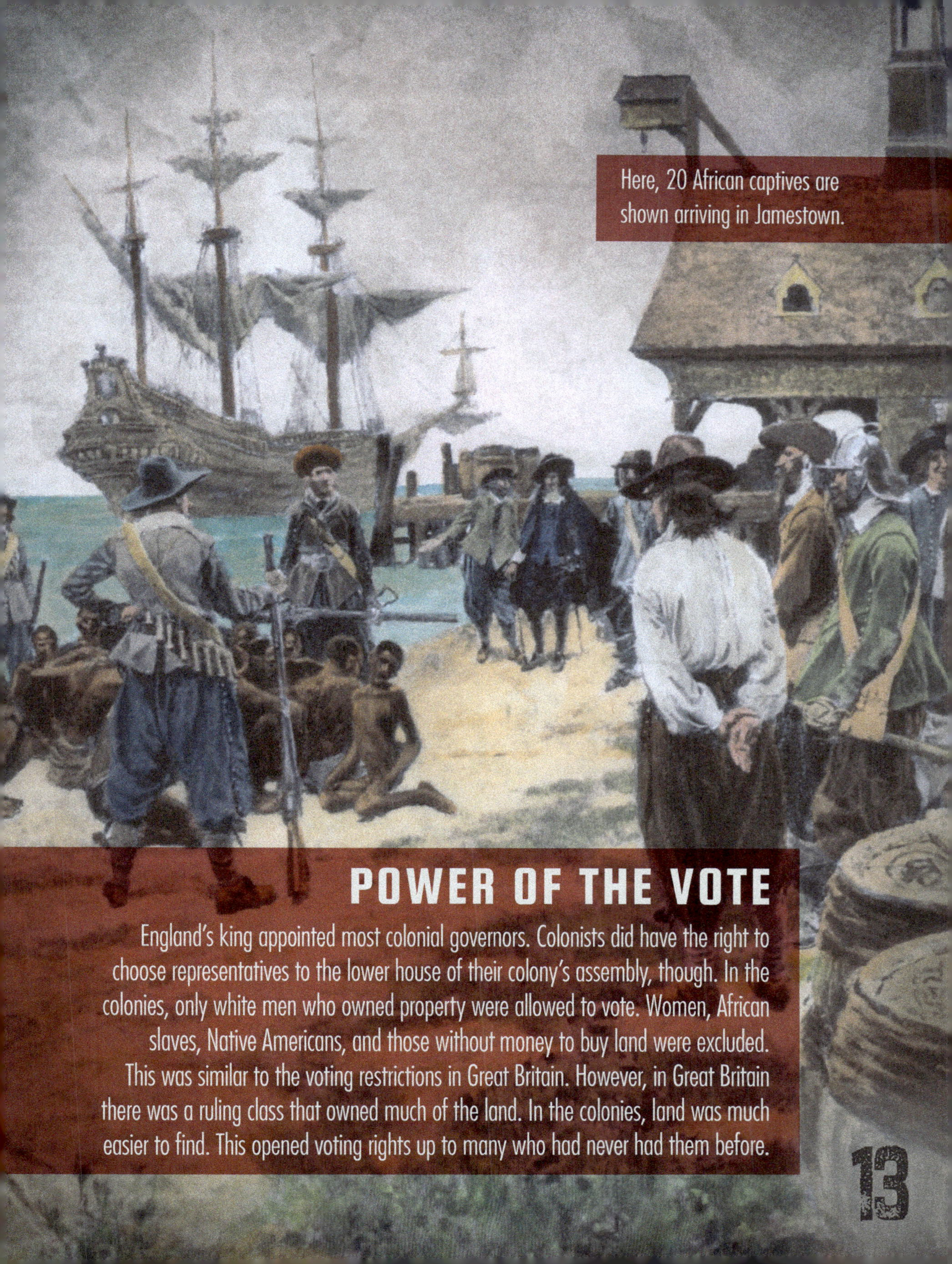

Here, 20 African captives are shown arriving in Jamestown.

POWER OF THE VOTE

England's king appointed most colonial governors. Colonists did have the right to choose representatives to the lower house of their colony's assembly, though. In the colonies, only white men who owned property were allowed to vote. Women, African slaves, Native Americans, and those without money to buy land were excluded. This was similar to the voting restrictions in Great Britain. However, in Great Britain there was a ruling class that owned much of the land. In the colonies, land was much easier to find. This opened voting rights up to many who had never had them before.

THE FRENCH AND INDIAN WAR

While England established colonies along the Atlantic coast, other European countries claimed their own lands in North America. Spain controlled Florida and several Caribbean islands. France held several settlements in modern-day Canada. They also controlled the land west of the 13 colonies up to the Mississippi River. This land was called New France and very few people lived there. As England and France both tried to expand their territory, tensions between the two countries rose.

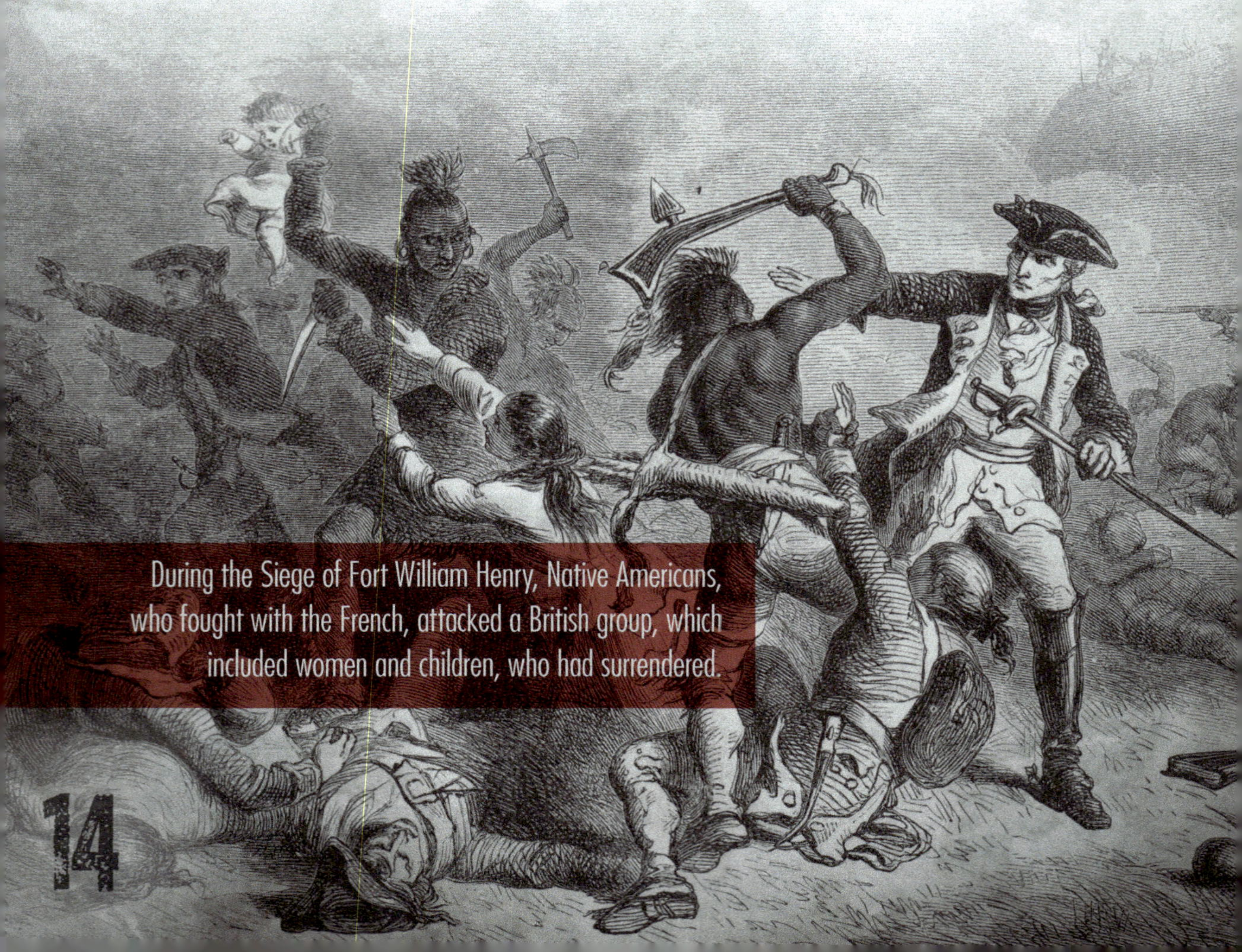

During the Siege of Fort William Henry, Native Americans, who fought with the French, attacked a British group, which included women and children, who had surrendered.

The lands of New France and the British colonies lay very close to each other and there were sometimes disagreements about who owned certain areas. The Ohio River Valley was one area in dispute. The French had built several military forts there. In 1754, colonial forces tried to capture the land, but the French defeated them. Both the British and French governments reacted, and fighting began in what the colonists called the French and Indian War, named for their French enemies and France's Native American allies. After several defeats by the French, the colonial forces gained control of the Ohio River Valley and areas of Canada, including Quebec. In 1763, France signed a **treaty** giving the land of New France to the British. Spain, which had helped France, agreed to hand over Florida to the British in exchange for Cuba.

The French and Indian War was of great importance to the colonists. In Europe, however, the fighting was a small part of a much larger conflict called the Seven Years' War. Great Britain and its allies fought against France, Austria, Russia, Sweden, and Saxony in the long, expensive war.

After the French and Indian War, Great Britain had a lot more territory in North America. However, this new territory contained French-Canadians and many Native Americans, some of whom had supported Great Britain and some who had supported France.

GEORGE WASHINGTON

One of the men who tried to capture the Ohio River Valley for the British was a young officer named George Washington (1732–1799). He would go on to command the Continental Army against the British during the American Revolution. His knowledge of the British Army's strengths, weaknesses, and tactics would be a big advantage to the colonial forces.

DIFFERING INTERESTS

At first, the treaty signed by France to end the French and Indian War seemed a success to the colonists. They no longer had to worry about attacks from French forces. Great Britain also expanded its territory, which the colonists believed would give them more land on which to settle. However, the treaty and the end results of the war would lead to greater problems between the colonists and the British crown.

The Seven Years' War and the French and Indian War had put Great Britain deep into debt. The British government had also decided to keep about 10,000 British soldiers in the colonies to protect against attacks by Native Americans. This standing army would cost the British even more money. Britain's prime minister George Grenville (1712–1770) believed that, since the army's main role was to protect the colonies, the colonists should contribute in some way to the cost. His solution was to create new **taxes** on the colonies and raise taxes already in place.

By 1763, a law called the Molasses Act was about to expire. The act put a 6-pence per gallon tax on molasses imported, or brought in, from non-British colonies, such as the French West Indies. However, the tax was rarely collected. To replace the Molasses Act and raise revenue, or money, the British passed the Sugar Act in 1764. The Sugar Act lowered the tax on imported molasses to 3-pence per gallon, but also made sure that the tax would actually be collected.

In 1765, Great Britain passed another act that would prove unpopular. The Stamp Act required colonists to pay a tax on printed materials, including legal documents and newspapers. The Sugar Act and Stamp Act angered many colonists. They were the first taxes placed on the colonies that seemed designed only to raise money instead of regulating trade. Many colonists were growing uneasy with the way that Great Britain was governing them and the precedent that these taxes set.

This satirical illustration shows a funeral procession for the unpopular Stamp Act, representing its repeal in 1766.

MORE TAXES

The Sugar Act raised taxes on goods besides molasses, such as sugar, coffee, wine, and some fabrics. These products were very important to the colonies, and the higher costs threatened many businesses.

TAXATION

In the United States today, people sometimes take it for granted that individual citizens have a voice in government. People have the right to vote in elections that decide who will make local, state, and federal laws. Each state has two representatives in the U.S. Senate and a certain number of representatives in the House of Representatives. The people in each state vote for who will represent them in these houses at a national level. Each state also has its own **legislature**, made up of representatives elected by the people of the state.

After the passing of the Stamp Act, many colonists began to protest the new taxes. The Virginia legislature, called the House of Burgesses, decided that the British **Parliament** did not have the right to impose taxes on the colonies. They believed the colonists had the right to only be taxed by their own representatives, and that residents of Virginia should not have to pay any taxes except those passed by the House of Burgesses.

Opposition to the Stamp Act was soon uniting the 13 colonies in a way that other issues had not. In October 1765, a few days before the Stamp Act was to take effect, a group of **delegates** from nine of the 13 colonies met in New York City to discuss the issue. The meeting was called the Stamp Act Congress. The delegates signed a **petition** to King George III (1738–1820) and the British parliament declaring that they did not have the right to tax the colonies because the colonists did not have the right to vote and send a representative to Parliament.

It became clear to the British government that it would be more trouble than it was worth to enforce the Stamp Act. The Sugar Act and Stamp Act were repealed, or got rid of, in 1766. However, the British government still believed that they had the right to tax the colonies in any way they chose.

In a famous speech before the Second Virginia Convention in 1775, Patrick Henry declared, "Give me liberty, or give me death!"

BOSTON RIOTS

On August 14, 1765, a group of Boston merchants hung an effigy, or dummy, of the city's Stamp Act Commissioner from a tree. A crowd gathered and marched through the city, finally arriving at the stamp office and pulling the building down. The tree where the effigy was hung became a popular place for protest meetings and was called the Liberty Tree.

CHAPTER 3

TENSIONS ESCALATE

Tensions were running high between the colonists and the British government. Although the ideas of complete independence and war had not yet begun to take shape, both sides were reaching breaking point. The colonists felt more and more that their interests were not being considered in British government.

While the Sugar Act and Stamp Act had angered colonists and threatened to hurt them financially, another British law was causing concern, too. When the French signed over their territories in North America to Great Britain after the French and Indian War, the colonists were excited. They believed they would be able to move into these new lands and expand their settlements. However, the land was still occupied by Native American tribes, who had not been a part of any agreement. As white colonists moved into the land of the Appalachian Mountains, conflicts arose between the colonists and the Native Americans.

The British government wanted to satisfy both the colonists and the Native Americans and avoid another expensive war. They tried to stop colonists from moving into the new territories, but also refused to remove them once they were there. In response, a leader of the Ottawa tribe named Pontiac organized an attack on British forts. To avoid further fighting, the British enacted the Proclamation of 1763, which prevented the colonists from moving into any land west of Appalachia. Colonists who had bought land in the western territory were forced to withdraw.

A typical colonial house, similar to the reproduction shown here, would be filled with items built or sewn by its inhabitants.

HOMESPUN MOVEMENT

The Homespun Movement was an act of patriotism by colonial women. Instead of buying cloth from Great Britain, they spun and wove their own cloth. The women of the movement would later go on to make clothing and blankets for colonial soldiers during the war.

Until 1760, the colonies had been populated by people with very different interests. Great Britain's taxes and land policies had now served to unite many of them against the British government. Colonists responded to Britain's actions by **boycotting** British goods such as tea and cloth. They also began to see themselves in a new way, either as **Loyalists**, who sided with the British, or **Patriots**, who wanted change.

MASSACRE

In 1768, Great Britain passed a set of laws known as the Townshend Acts. This series of acts included new taxes on imported items such as glass, paint, paper, and tea. One of the main purposes of the Townshend Acts was to raise money to pay the salaries of colonial governors and judges, with the hope that they would remain loyal to Great Britain. The colonists saw the laws as another example of taxation without representation.

The Massachusetts House of Representatives sent a petition to George III asking that the Townshend Acts be repealed. They also asked the legislatures of other colonies to join them in their resistance. The British government was concerned by the actions of Massachusetts' legislature. They began sending military regiments to Boston. This further heightened tensions in the city.

On February 22, 1770, an 11-year-old boy named Christopher Seider (1758–1770) joined in a protest outside the home of a British customs employee. The mob threw stones at the employee's house, and he responded by firing his gun into the crowd, killing Seider. A large public funeral was held for Seider, and Samuel Adams (1722–1803) called him "the first martyr to American liberty."

In the days after Seider's death, angry colonists harassed British soldiers. On the evening of March 5, a small group of men began arguing with a British soldier stationed outside the Custom House. The soldier struck one of the men in the head with his musket. This attracted a crowd of colonists. As the evening went on, the crowd grew larger. Church bells, which at the time were often used to signal a fire, were rung, which brought out even more people. More soldiers arrived. In the noise and confusion, the soldiers fired into the crowd of colonists, killing five men.

PROPAGANDA WAR

A few weeks after the events of the Boston Massacre, Paul Revere (1735–1818) published an engraving in the *Boston Gazette* showing a British captain giving a signal to the soldiers to fire. Other published accounts described the massacre as an organized attack by the soldiers on a peaceful crowd. However, some who supported the British claimed that the colonists had ambushed the soldiers, who feared an attack by the angry mob. The stories spread and helped shape many peoples' opinions about going to war.

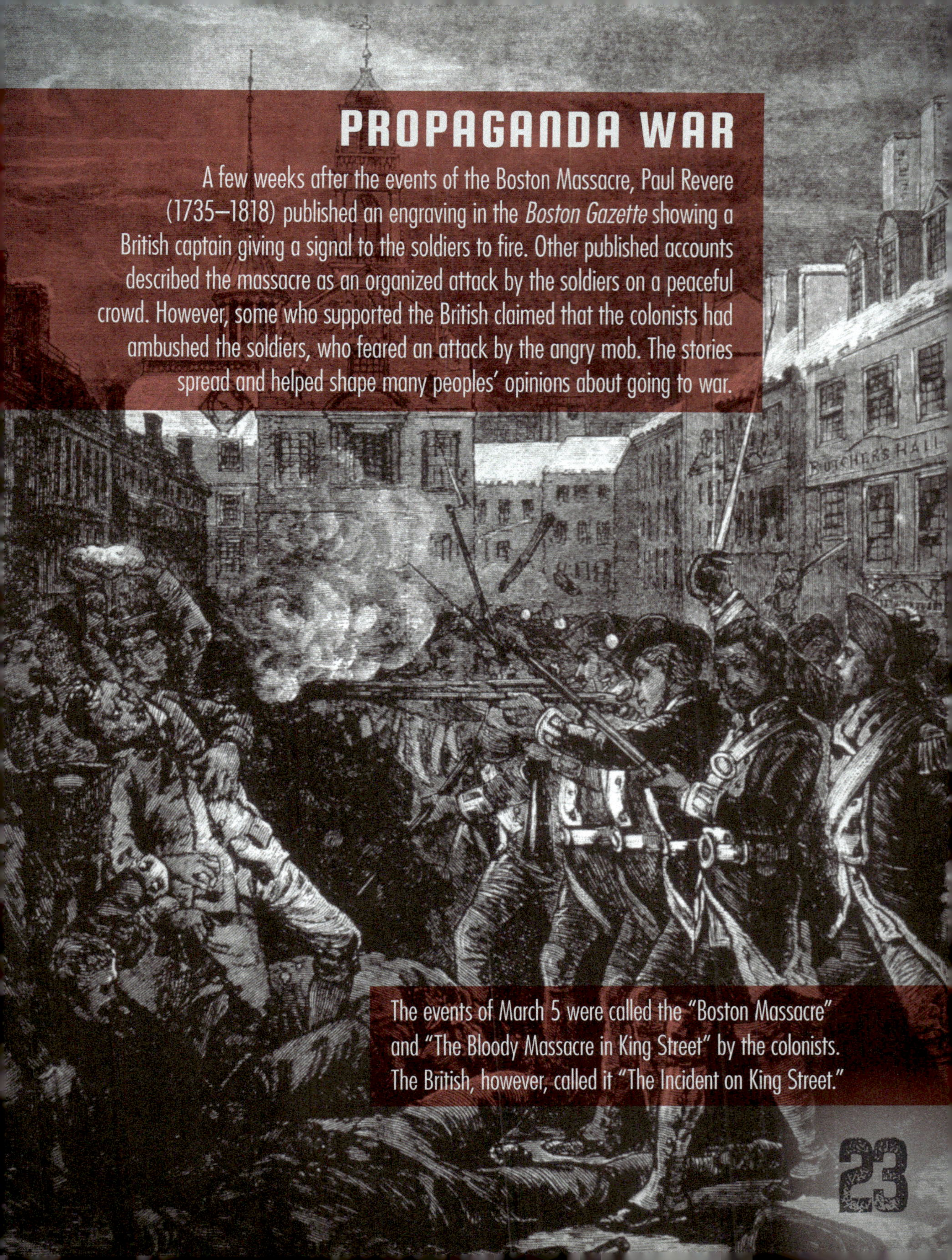

The events of March 5 were called the "Boston Massacre" and "The Bloody Massacre in King Street" by the colonists. The British, however, called it "The Incident on King Street."

THE BOSTON TEA PARTY

Boston remained a center of colonial rebellion. In 1773, another British law, called the Tea Act, once again set off tensions in the city and throughout the colonies.

The British East India Company was a very old British company that traded many goods, including silk, cotton, salt, and tea. Many wealthy people in Great Britain owned a part of the company. Before the Tea Act was passed in 1773, the British East Indian Company had to sell the tea they owned at an auction in London. However, after the French and Indian War, a lot of Europe was deep in debt, and tea sales were suffering. At the time the act was passed, the British East India Company owned 17 million pounds (7.71 million kg) of unsold tea. The passage of the Tea Act allowed the company to import their tea to the American colonies and sell it at a very reduced price. Other colonial tea importers could not compete with this low cost.

For many colonists, the Tea Act was an insult. When ships carrying the British East India Company's tea arrived in New York and Philadelphia, colonists forced the ships to return to England. In the city of Charleston, the tea was unloaded, but left on the docks to rot. In Boston, however, the governor refused to allow ships to return to England and colonists refused to allow the tea to be unloaded.
On December 16, about 7,000 colonists gathered at a meeting over the issue of the tea. That evening, a group of colonists named the **Sons of Liberty** dressed themselves as Native Americans. They crept aboard the three ships docked in Boston Harbor and dumped 342 crates of tea into the water, destroying it.
The event eventually became known as the Boston Tea Party.

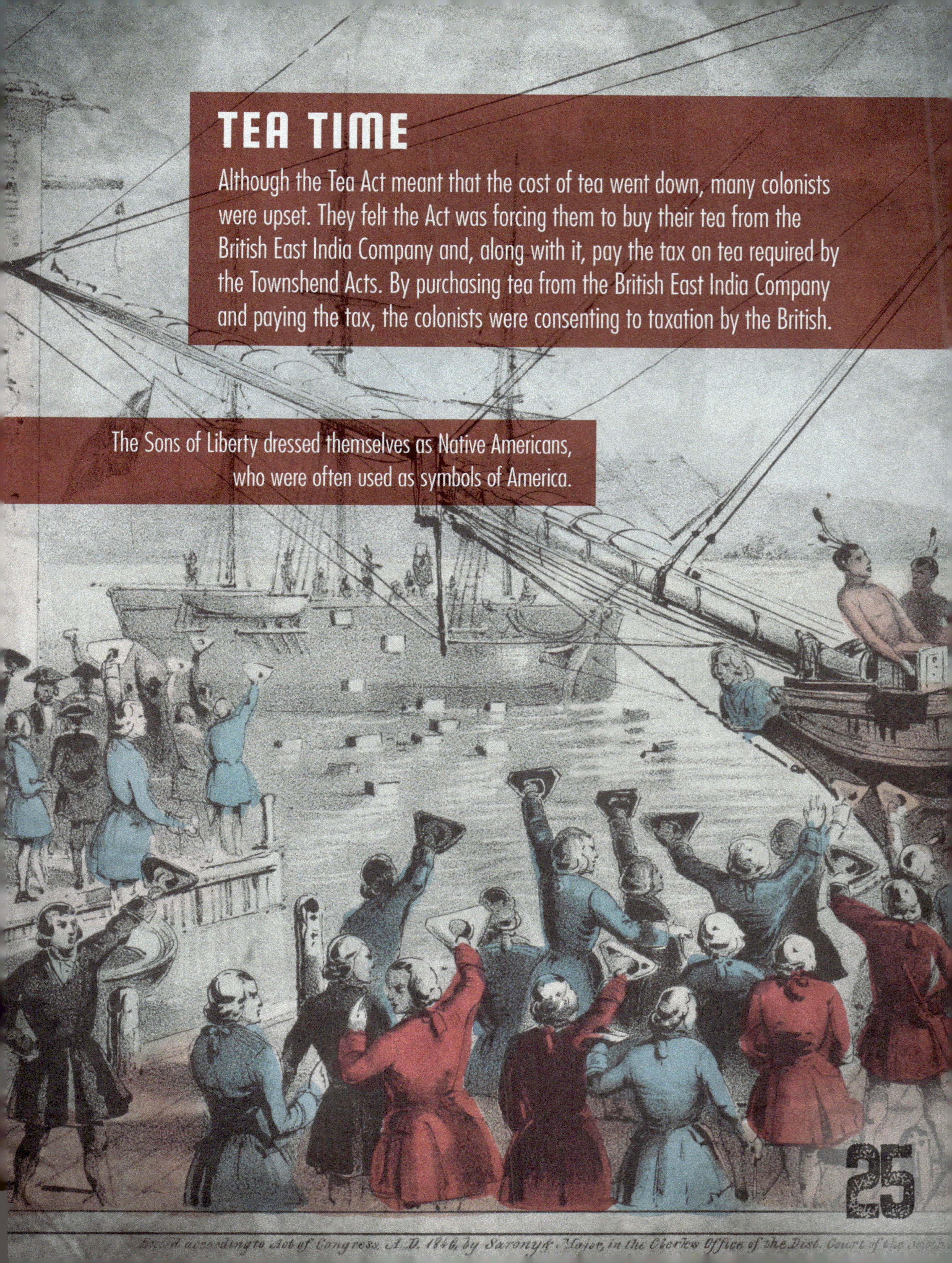

TEA TIME

Although the Tea Act meant that the cost of tea went down, many colonists were upset. They felt the Act was forcing them to buy their tea from the British East India Company and, along with it, pay the tax on tea required by the Townshend Acts. By purchasing tea from the British East India Company and paying the tax, the colonists were consenting to taxation by the British.

The Sons of Liberty dressed themselves as Native Americans, who were often used as symbols of America.

INTOLERABLE ACTS

Before the events of the Boston Tea Party, there were members of the British government who were sympathetic to the colonists. However, when news of the destruction reached London, the British government was united in its anger. They wanted to punish those responsible and bring the colonies back under British authority.

As punishment, the British government passed a group of five laws in 1774. The British called these laws the Coercive Acts or the Intolerable Acts. The first act closed Boston Harbor to all ships until the British East India Company had been repaid for the 342 crates of tea destroyed during the Boston Tea Party. The harbor was a major source of supplies, and its closure angered both Patriots and Loyalists.

The second act attempted to change the government of Massachusetts. It required nearly all appointments to governing positions in the Massachusetts Bay colony to be made by the governor, the king, or parliament. It also limited the number of town meetings Massachusetts colonists could hold to just one per year. This act caused a lot of concern throughout the colonies. They worried that the British might suddenly also control their governments.

Royal Navy ships patrolled the mouth of Boston Harbor to prevent any ships from entering.

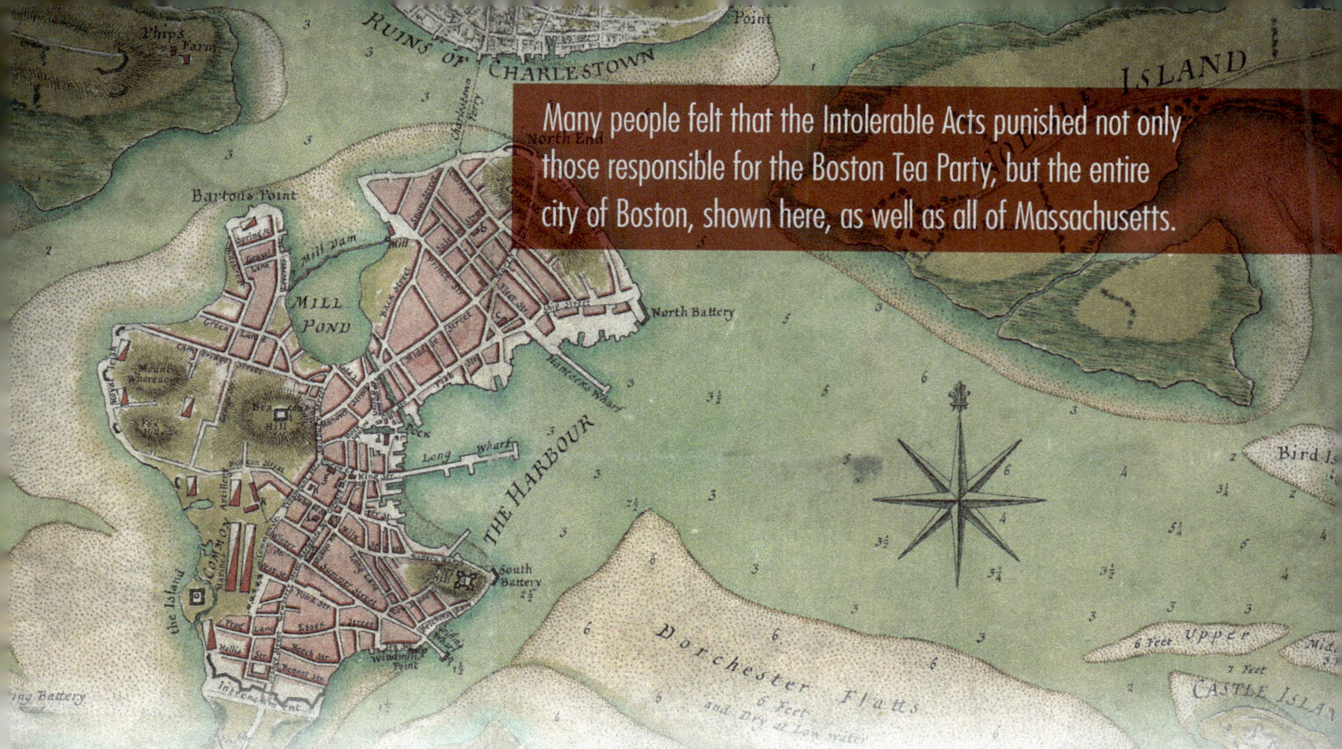

Many people felt that the Intolerable Acts punished not only those responsible for the Boston Tea Party, but the entire city of Boston, shown here, as well as all of Massachusetts.

The third act allowed the governor of a colony, who was appointed by the king, to move the trial of a royal official to another colony or even back to England if he believed the official would not get a fair trial in that colony. Witnesses would be reimbursed, or repaid, for their travel expenses if they went to England to testify. They would not be reimbursed for the time they lost at work, though, which made it unlikely that many would be able to make the long journey. Many felt this law would allow British officials to escape justice.

The fourth act allowed British troops to stay in the homes of colonists and other buildings.

BENEFITS FOR QUEBEC

The fifth act of the Intolerable Acts offered French residents of Quebec civil government and religious freedom. Though not directly related to the American colonies, many colonists considered it an insult.

CHAPTER 4

BEGINNINGS OF WAR

The Intolerable Acts were meant to stop the rebellious colonists and restore British rule and authority. Instead, they backfired, bringing the two sides closer to war. The acts angered the colonists and convinced more people that a solution needed to be found, and that independence from Great Britain might be the only answer.

In response to the Intolerable Acts, the colonists organized a meeting called the First Continental Congress. Its goal was to show Great Britain that the colonies were united and to resolve any issues between the colonies. From September 5 to October 16, 1774, representatives from 12 of the 13 colonies met in Pennsylvania.

Fifty-six delegates attended the meeting, including people such as George Washington, Patrick Henry (1736–1799), and John Adams (1735–1826). All agreed that a solution must be found to end the problems between the British government and the colonies. Not everyone agreed what that solution should be. Some, such as the delegates from New York and Pennsylvania, wanted to convince Great Britain to repeal the Intolerable Acts and find a peaceful solution to the conflict. Others wanted to remain British colonies, but find a way to be represented in Parliament. Others wanted to cut ties with the British and become independent.

After more than a month of discussion, the congress passed the Continental Association, which was a pact to boycott British goods. They sent a petition to King George III asking him to repeal the Intolerable Acts. They also made a plan to meet the following year if the acts were not repealed.

Patrick Henry, a lawyer and statesman from Virginia, was an outspoken member of the First Continental Congress.

GEORGIA OPTS OUT

The Colony of Georgia chose not to send any delegates to the First Continental Congress. At the time, they were involved in a conflict with Creek Indians, who were angry about being forced from their lands. Georgia did not want to upset the British, as they were dependent on them for military supplies. However, angered by the terms of the peace treaty between the Creeks and the royal governor, Georgia joined the other colonies in their rebellion just weeks after the end of the First Continental Congress.

THE FIRST SHOTS

Great Britain and its American colonies had been arguing for years over issues of taxes, trade, and representation in government. Even at the meeting of the First Continental Congress, though, war did not seem inevitable. Most delegates, and most of the colonists they represented, still hoped to find a peaceful resolution with Great Britain. The delegates planned to meet again, in May 1775, to discuss further steps if the British government did not meet their demands. However, before that meeting could take place, the first shots of the American Revolution were fired.

In August 1774, a group of Massachusetts Patriots met in Boston to discuss their opposition to the Massachusetts Government Act. This was the second act of the Intolerable Acts that essentially put the Massachusetts government under British control. The group passed the Suffolk Resolves, which was a pact to boycott British goods, pay no taxes to Great Britain, and disobey the Massachusetts Government Act. The Suffolk Resolves also encouraged the formation of **militias**, or groups of volunteer or citizen soldiers.

"PAUL REVERE'S RIDE"

The night before the battles of Lexington and Concord (see right), the colonists received information that the British were on their way to arrest Samuel Adams and John Hancock (1737–1793). Paul Revere and William Dawes (1745–1799) rode off to warn them and alert nearby militias. Almost a century later, Henry Wadsworth Longfellow (1807–1882) commemorated Paul Revere's midnight ride in a famous poem.

In response to the Suffolk Resolves, Great Britain declared Massachusetts to be in state of rebellion. In April 1775, British troops were given orders to destroy supplies being held by the militia in the town of Concord. They were also told to capture Samuel Adams and John Hancock, who were considered leaders of the rebellion. On April 19, in Lexington, the British troops met the small local militia of 77 men. The militia had been warned that the British were coming. Neither side expected a battle. However, a shot was fired, and the British attacked. The colonists retreated, and the British moved on to Concord. Outside Concord more members of the militia gathered, and more shots were fired. This time, the British retreated.

The colonial militia met about 700 British soldiers at the Battle of Lexington. Even today, no one knows which side fired the first shot of the battle.

A HISTORY OF REVOLT

Once the American Revolution had officially begun with the first shots fired in Lexington, it lasted nearly eight years. Over those years, the British and Americans met in battles big and small.

The key events of the war:

1775

April 19 The American Revolution officially begins.

May 10 The Americans win the Battle of Fort Ticonderoga.

June 17 The Battle of Bunker Hill results in a win for the British.

1776

July 4 The Continental Congress **ratifies** the Declaration of Independence.

August 27 George Washington's troops are defeated in the Battle of Long Island.

1777

October 17 The Battle of Saratoga comes to an end with the surrender of 7,000 British troops.

1778

September 27 British forces attack Continental troops in the Baylor Massacre.

1780

May 12 The British capture the city of Charleston, South Carolina.

1781

October 19 The Siege of Yorktown, the last major battle of the war, comes to an end when British General Charles Cornwallis (1738–1805) surrenders to George Washington.

1783

September 3 The American Revolution ends with the signing of the Treaty of Paris.

Although the colonial forces lost the Battle of Bunker Hill, the heavy losses suffered by the British were a big confidence boost for the colonists.

CHAPTER 5

FORMING A NEW NATION

The plans for the Second Continental Congress to meet had been made in the fall of 1774, before the battles of Lexington and Concord. If not for the events at Lexington and Concord, what might the Second Continental Congress have looked like? Could war have been avoided if the delegates had continued with their plan of boycotts and petitions? When the time came for the Second Continental Congress to meet in May 1775, things had changed. The Americans and the British were at war.

Many of the delegates from the First Continental Congress also attended the Second Continental Congress. A delegate from Virginia named Peyton Randolph (1721–1775), who had been appointed president of the first meeting, was appointed president once again, though he would later be replaced by newcomer John Hancock. Benjamin Franklin (1706–1790) attended the meeting for the first time.

When the Second Continental Congress began, its goals were different than those of the first meeting. Many of the delegates still wanted to find a peaceful solution that would allow the colonies to remain under the British crown without further loss of life. A growing number believed complete independence was the only answer. Still, the colonies were at war and someone had to take command of the war effort. On June 14, the Continental Army was created and George Washington was appointed as commanding general. Washington had served as a senior officer on the side of British during the French and Indian War, and his knowledge of British tactics and weaknesses would prove valuable to the Patriots.

THE OLIVE BRANCH PETITION

On July 8, 1775, the Second Continental Congress sent a document called the Olive Branch Petition to London. The petition was a last chance at avoiding war and making peace with Great Britain. It explained that the colonists did not want full independence and wished to remain loyal to the king. However, around that same time, the British intercepted a letter from John Adams to a friend. This letter spoke of war being inevitable and the capture of British officials. After hearing about this, King George III refused to read the Olive Branch Petition, and the colonies had their answer.

INDEPENDENCE!

When the First and Second Continental Congresses were organized, they were intended to be a way for delegates from each of the colonies to come together and discuss issues. They were also meant to speak as a collective voice for the colonists when dealing with the British government. However, as the American Revolution began, the members of the second Continental Congress began to act as the governing body of the colonies, though legally they had no standing as a government. To manage the war effort, they raised an army, printed money, signed treaties, and found ways to do what they believed needed to be done.

As the American Revolution went on, the Continental Congress realized that they would need help from other powers to defeat the British. However, the colonies still belonged to the crown, and the Congress knew no other European country would get involved in the conflict while the colonists were under British control. The solution they found was to declare themselves an independent country.

On June 11, 1776, the Congress appointed a group called the Committee of Five to write the declaration. The members of the committee, or group, were Thomas Jefferson (1743–1826), Roger Sherman (1721–1793), Benjamin Franklin, John Adams, and Robert R. Livingston (1746–1813). It was decided that Thomas Jefferson should write a **draft**, or a first version, of the declaration. When he was finished, the draft was brought to the other members of the committee to be discussed and changed as necessary. The Committee of Five worked on another draft, and then presented it to the other delegates on June 28. More changes were suggested and added. On July 2, the Congress voted to pass the Declaration of Independence. Two days later, on July 4, the document was printed for the general public to see.

IN CONGRESS, JULY 4, 1776.

The unanimous Declaration of the thirteen united States of America,

The Declaration of Independence, seen here, was signed by 56 delegates.

IMPORTANT SIGNATURES

One month after the passing of the Declaration of Independence, on August 2, delegates met to sign the document. John Dickinson (1732–1808), who had led the writing of the Olive Branch Petition and had pushed for reconciliation with the British, refused to sign. Others signed even though they had voted against the declaration. Though they did not agree with the idea of becoming an independent country, they recognized the importance of showing the British government a united front.

LASTING FRAMEWORK

Before the American Revolution, each colony had acted independently of the others. While the colonies were at war, a government was needed to make important decisions and organize the war effort. The Continental Congress created a document that would act as a framework for a new government. This document, written in 1776, and adopted by the Continental Congress on November 15, 1777, was called the Articles of Confederation.

The Articles of Confederation was a pact, or agreement, between the 13 colonies. It formed a weak central government and gave the Congress permission to make agreements, or treaties, with countries in Europe and with Native Americans. It gave most other rights to the individual colonies. It dealt with how each colony would

George Washington presided over the convention created to replace the Articles of Confederation in 1787.

vote to pass laws that applied to the entire group. It also stated that all 13 colonies had to agree before the Articles of Confederation could be amended, or changed.

The Articles of Confederation was ratified, or officially agreed to, by the last of the 13 colonies in February 1781. Just one year later, in February 1782, the British Parliament voted to end the war. Their defeat at the Siege of Yorktown had convinced many in the country that they should stop fighting. Peace talks between the two sides began, with Benjamin Franklin, John Adams, and Henry Laurens (1724–1792) representing the Americans. On September 3, 1783, nearly a year and a half later, the Treaty of Paris was signed, officially ending the American Revolution.

When the war was over and the United States began to fully function as a country, the problems with the Articles of Confederation became more and more apparent. Congress could pass laws, but had no power or structure to force states to follow them. Congress also did not have the power to collect taxes from the states. It could only ask the states for money, requests that the states often refused or ignored. This led to a serious lack of funding. It was soon decided that a new framework was needed if the United States was to succeed as a country.

FRIENDSHIP BETWEEN THE COLONIES

The Articles of Confederation dealt mainly with agreements between the colonies. It allowed people to pass freely between the colonies and said that criminals fleeing to another colony would be returned to the colony of the crime to stand trial. It also stated that if one colony was attacked, the others would help.

CHAPTER 6

LEGACY AND LESSONS

For years, the colonists and the British had been engaged in a bloody war. Many families lost husbands, fathers, and sons. However, with all that was lost, something was gained. The leaders of the United States worked together to shape a new country and create a framework for its government. This document, the **U.S. Constitution**, has lasted for more than 200 years and has been a model for countries all around the world.

After the failures of the Articles of Confederation, a convention was called to create a new framework. For four months in 1787, delegates met in Philadelphia, debating different ideas of government and making **compromises**. They knew the United States needed a stronger central government than the Articles of Confederation had created. However, they did not want individual states or people to lose their rights. Finally, on September 17, 1787, the delegates signed the Constitution. It was then sent to each state for ratification. Nine states needed to ratify the Constitution before it would become official. The ninth state ratified the Constitution on June 21, 1788, and it took effect in 1789. By 1790, the thirteenth and final state, Rhode Island, ratified the document.

The Constitution had been approved by all 13 states. However, there were still people who believed that some changes needed to be made. Many believed that the Constitution did not go far enough to protect certain freedoms.

To fix this, 10 amendments, or changes, were added to the Constitution in 1791. These 10 amendments are called the Bill of Rights. They ensure the protection of many of the rights that we sometimes take for granted today, such as the freedom of speech, freedom of religion, and the right to a trial by jury.

THE GREAT COMPROMISE

One issue that divided the delegates was how many votes each state would get in the U.S. Congress. Larger states wanted the number of votes to be based on population. Smaller states wanted every state to get the same number of votes. Delegate Roger Sherman suggested that there should be two houses in Congress. In one, the Senate, each state would get the same number of votes. In the other, the House of Representatives, votes would be based on population. The plan was known as the Great Compromise.

The Constitution was originally composed of a preamble and seven articles.

REPRESENTATION AND RIGHTS

The American Revolution was fought for many reasons. One of the strongest was the colonists' belief that they did not have a voice in the British Parliament and that they were unfairly being taxed without representation. When the Founding Fathers had the chance to create a framework for the new government of the United States, they made sure that the country's citizens would be represented.

The U.S. Constitution is not a long document, but it lays the framework for how our government is still organized and run today. The central government, called the federal government, is divided into three branches. These are called the legislative, executive, and judicial branches. The legislative branch includes the Congress and makes the laws. The executive branch includes the president and enforces the laws. The judicial branch, which includes the Supreme Court, interprets the laws. By dividing the government into three branches, the Constitution allows

FUTURE LEADERS

The people who fought in and led others during the American Revolution would go on to shape the early history of the United States. Some, such as George Washington, John Adams, and Thomas Jefferson, would go on to serve as U.S. President. The lessons they learned during the war had an important effect on how they later served and on the creation of our modern country.

The Supreme Court is currently made up of nine justices. They are nominated by the president and confirmed by the Senate.

no one person or group to become too powerful. In addition, all offices in the government are filled with people who have been elected by the people, or appointed by someone who has been elected.

To look back at the American Revolution today, what lessons were learned? In the years before the war, Great Britain was one of the most powerful countries in the world, with a colonial empire stretching around the globe. However, under the right circumstances, a small group of ill-prepared colonists were able to win their freedom. While losing the American colonies was not a devastating loss to Great Britain, it was an important lesson to the British Parliament, as well as those under colonial rule around the world, that the British Empire was not bulletproof.

THE LEGACY

The effects of the American Revolution are felt in the United States every day, from the structure of our government to the freedoms and rights we enjoy. The effects of the war were not confined to the United States, though. The American Revolution influenced other movements around the world, whose effects are also still felt today.

The most important event on which the American Revolution had an influence was likely the French Revolution. Many of the ideas written about by the Founding Fathers, such as equality, liberty, and the basic rights of man, actually had their roots in French thinking. The American Revolution showed the French that these ideas could be a reality and that a powerful government could be overthrown. In 1789, ordinary French citizens revolted and overthrew their king and ruling class. The French Revolution had massive and lasting effects on all of Europe.

One motto of the French Revolution translates in English as "Liberty, Equality, Fraternity."

In her left hand, the Statue of Liberty holds a tablet inscribed with the date of July 4, 1776.

IRISH REBELLION OF 1798

The American and French revolutions also had an effect on a rebellion in Ireland in 1798. A group called the United Irishmen had been heavily influenced by both revolutions and by the new government of the United States. Their goal was an independent Ireland, completely separate from England. Unlike the American and French revolutions, though, the Irish Rebellion was ultimately unsuccessful, and Ireland was brought under even tighter British control.

No war happens for just one single reason. Most are the result of years of tension and buildup. The American Revolution was no different. Looking back, there seem to be many moments when war might have been avoided. We can ask ourselves, what if the British government had offered the colonists a voice in Parliament? What may have happened if no shots had been fired at the Battle of Lexington? Would the United States, in its current form, exist today? Would the world be a very different place? There is no way to know for sure. By learning about what caused the American Revolution, though, we can examine the motivations of the people involved and understand more about the birth of our country.

GLOSSARY

boycotting joining with others in refusing to buy from or deal with a person, nation, or business

charter an official agreement giving someone permission to do something

colonies places ruled by leaders of another country

compromises to give things to reach agreements

debt something owed

delegates representatives elected to attend a political gathering

draft a nonfinal version of a document

legislature a body of people that has the power to make or pass laws

Loyalists people who were faithful to the British Crown

militias groups of volunteer or citizen soldiers who are organized to assemble in emergencies

natural resources things in nature that can be used by people

Ottoman Empire the Turkish empire in the thirteenth century that included parts of Asia and southeast Europe

Parliament the group in Great Britain that made the country's laws

Patriots American colonists who believed in separating from British rule

petition a formal way to ask for something to be done

ratifies approve officially

Sons of Liberty a group of American colonists who protested the British government's taxes and unfair treatment

taxes money added to the price of something or paid to a government

treaty an official agreement, signed and agreed upon by each party

U.S. Constitution the document that explains the different parts of the nation's government and how each part works

FOR MORE INFORMATION

BOOKS

Burgan, Michael. *The Split History of the American Revolution* (Perspectives Flip Books). North Mankato, MN: Compass Point Books, 2013.

Cook, Peter. *You Wouldn't Want to Be at the Boston Tea Party!: Wharf Water Tea You'd Rather Not Drink*. Danbury, CT: Franklin Watts, 2014.

Schanzer, Rosalyn. *George vs. George: The American Revolution as Seen from Both Sides.* Washington, DC: National Geographic Children's Books, 2007.

WEBSITES

Click through the "Boston Tea Party History" and "American Revolution History" links at:

www.bostonteapartyship.com

Investigate the discovery of North America, including some short movies at:

www.history.com/topics/exploration/exploration-of-north-america

Discover a detailed chronicle of the Revolution at:

www.pbs.org/ktca/liberty/chronicle.html

Take a look at daily life around the time of the first Thanksgiving at:

www.scholastic.com/scholastic_thanksgiving/daily_life

Publisher's note to educators and parents: Our editors have carefully reviewed these websites to ensure that they are suitable for students. Many websites change frequently, however, and we cannot guarantee that a site's future contents will continue to meet our high standards of quality and educational value. Be advised that students should be closely supervised whenever they access the Internet.

INDEX